The Origins of Wisdom

ZEN BUDDHISM

O. B. DUANE

Copyright © 1997 Brockhampton Press

First published in Great Britain in 1997 by
Brockhampton Press,
20 Bloomsbury Street,
London WC1B 3QA
A member of the Hodder Headline Group.

ISBN 1 86019 551 2

A copy of the C.I.P. data is available from
the British Library upon request.

Produced for Brockhampton Press by Flame Tree Publishing,
a part of The Foundry Creative Media Company Limited,
The Long House, Antrobus Road, Chiswick, London W4 5HY

The Origins of Wisdom

ZEN BUDDHISM

O. B. DUANE

BROCKHAMPTON PRESS

Foreword

❉

OF ALL THE EASTERN spiritual philosophies, techniques and practices which have made their way West into Europe and North America during the past century, Zen Buddhism has fascinated Western culture perhaps more than any other. The word Zen has worked its way into our language, Zen abbeys and monasteries have sprung up from Cumbria to the Hollywood Hills, and a huge range of modern thinkers – from the great psychologist C. G. Jung to the poets of the 'Beat Generation' – have been drawn to Zen and to the possibilities of simplicity, spontaneity, and deep spiritual insight which it offers.

As well as being fascinating, however, Zen is also one of the most challenging spiritual paths since it refuses to be contained by any intellectual formula or system of belief. Rather it asks us to stop trying to intellectualize and define, and to concentrate on the pure, living experience of the moment. An introduction to the subject of Zen Buddhism like this book, cannot offer us an easy definition of Zen, because no easy definition exists, but it can guide us into the world of Zen thought and practice – a world which is difficult, sometimes confusing, but never dry or stale; always fascinating and always rewarding.

Alex Gooch, MA
January 1997

Zen Buddhism is an attitude and a way of life, the essence of which is to realize the mind of the Buddha.

Contents

Introduction

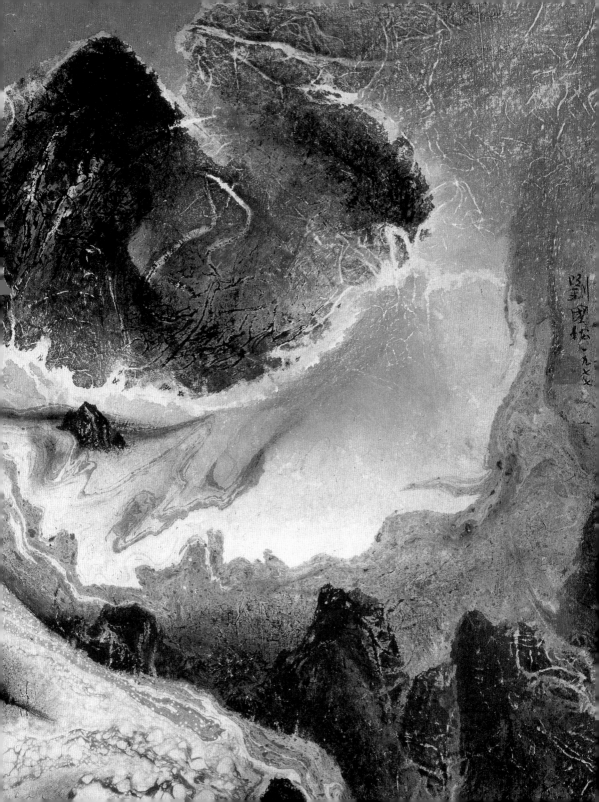

Introduction

✤

Sentient beings are numberless; I vow to save them.
Desires are inexhaustible; I vow to extinguish them.
Dharmas are boundless; I vow to master them.
The Buddha Way is unsurpassable; I vow to attain it.

The Four Great Vows of Zen, recited after every meditation.

IT WOULD NOT BE ENTIRELY ACCURATE to describe Zen Buddhism as a religion, since its followers neither affirm nor deny the existence of God. It would be better described as a movement. The essence of Zen Buddhism is to realize the mind of the Buddha, yet there is no formulated doctrine or theological thought process by which to approach Zen. It is an attitude, a way and a view of life which leads to a sense of personal liberation and, as such, it does not readily fit into any of the modern Western categories of religion, philosophy, psychology or science.

The word Zen is the Japanese equivalent of the Sanskrit *dhyana*, usually translated as the 'meditation' of Mahayana Buddhism. In China, this movement is known as 'Ch'an'. Zen makes such statements as 'willows are green, flowers are red', or 'fire is hot, water is cold'. These are such ordinary observations that to

In Japan, many elements of Zen teaching affect the lives of ordinary people.

place emphasis on them appears slightly bewildering, especially to the Western mind. Zen also offers such paradoxical sayings as 'a bridge flows, whereas water does not flow', 'the blue mountains are constantly walking', or 'the stone woman gives birth to a child at night'. Zen therefore embodies both self-evident and illogical modes of expression which characterize it as something beyond intellectual analysis. It is not in itself a philosophy, but it does embrace a profound philosophy which is based upon 'Self-Awakening'.

Enlightenment comes from practice,
Thus Enlightenment is limitless;
Practice comes from Enlightenment,
Thus practice has no beginning.

Dogen Zenji

The philosophy of Zen is firmly rooted in the concept of non-thinking and implies a rejection of all conceptual media or methods. There is a well-known Zen story which teaches that the Buddha preached for forty-nine years and yet his 'broad tongue' did not move once. 'The instant you speak about it, you miss the mark,' declared the Buddha. There is nothing to explain by words or theory; Zen always expresses the 'unspeakable', a reality which is beyond negation and affirmation, speech and silence. The ultimate goal in the practice of Zen and Buddhism is 'absolute nothingness' or 'emptiness'. Buddha-nature is without form or colour. It is limitless and boundless.

Words!
The Way is beyond language,
for in it there is
no yesterday
no tomorrow
no today.

Hsin-hsin Ming

The ultimate goal of the Zen practitioner is to achieve the state of Enlightenment experienced by the Buddha.

The Origins of Zen Buddhism

The Origins of Zen Buddhism

> **When we hit our two hands together, we hear a clap.**
> **Now listen to the sound of one hand clapping.**
>
> *Hakuin Zenji*

BUDDHISM FIRST ENTERED CHINA from India in the first century AD. Of any other alien influence, it had perhaps the most dramatic, long-term effect on the nation's culture, but this transformation was by no means immediate, and for centuries Buddhism encountered strong opposition, particularly from those supporting the practical philosophies of Confucianism. The Zen School of Buddhism, which has been described as a revolt against the intellectual Buddhism of India, was founded by Bodhidharma, the Twenty-eighth Patriarch of Buddhism, who arrived in China from India around the year AD 520. It is said that he was forced to withdraw to a monastery for a number of years, as he did not find favour with the Emperor. Bodhidharma had a disciple at this monastery known as Hui-K'o who subsequently became the Second Patriarch of Zen in China. The title

Opposite: *Bodhidarma founded the Zen School of Buddhism in China, after travelling there from India in AD 520.*
Overleaf: *The Eihei-Ji monastery, established by Dogen Zenji, founder of the Soto School, which still remains today.*

Patriarch is given to the first thirty-four Dharma successors from the Shakyamuni Buddha through to the Sixth Patriarch, Hui-neng. Nowadays, it is an honorary title used to describe a Zen master of outstanding attainment.

The Patriarchate ceased with the death of Hui-neng and his tradition passed to five disciples: Huai-jang (AD 775), Ch'ing-yuan (AD 740), Shen-hui (AD 668–770), Hsuan-chueh (AD 665–713), and Hui-chung (AD 677–744). The religious descendants of these disciples live on today in the two major schools of Zen in Japan, the Soto and the Rinzai.

Zen Schools

The Soto school of Zen Buddhism was introduced into Japan by Dogen Zenji, (b. AD 1200) who, at the age of fourteen, entered the great Tendai monastery at Mount Hiei with the principal object of finding the correct path to self-knowledge. There he studied under the revered master, Myozen, accompanying him to China in AD 1223 in search of the most authentic form of Buddhism. Following the death of Myozen, Dogen became a disciple of the Soto master, Nyojo, who taught him the difficult technique of sitting meditation known as *za-zen*. Dogen eventually established the great monastery of Eihei-ji which is still the principle Soto centre today.

Soto Zen evolved in Japan during a turbulent period of political corruption when the socio-economic system of the *shoen*, or feudal manor, encouraged routine exploitation of the peasants by the élite. The Soto school advocated the individuality of the person without reference to his social class, while at the same time cultivating meditative discipline. It emphasized two main points, the first, that there is no gap between Enlightenment and practice, and the second, that the correct mode of daily behaviour is Buddhism itself.

The Rinzai Zen school, whose founder was Rinzai Gigen (Chinese: Lin-chi I hsuan, d. AD 866), a great master of the Tang dynasty, has a somewhat different approach. This school of Zen is noted for its vigorous use of koans (discussions between master and pupil) in *za-zen* practice, and stresses that the achievement of Enlightenment *(satori)* is through the use of the koans. The Rinzai School of Zen was introduced into Japan in AD 1191 by the Japanese Tendai monk, Eisai (AD 1141–1215), who established monasteries at Kyoto and Kamakura under the patronage of the Emperor.

Both schools of Zen Buddhism, each with a different opinion as to whether Enlightenment is a slow or spontaneous development, have contributed greatly to the culture of Japan. Zen has penetrated almost every aspect of Japanese life, from architecture, poetry, painting and the crafts, to trading, athletics and the Japanese language itself.

Mount Hiei. On this mountain is the great Tendai monastery, where Dogen Zenji studied.

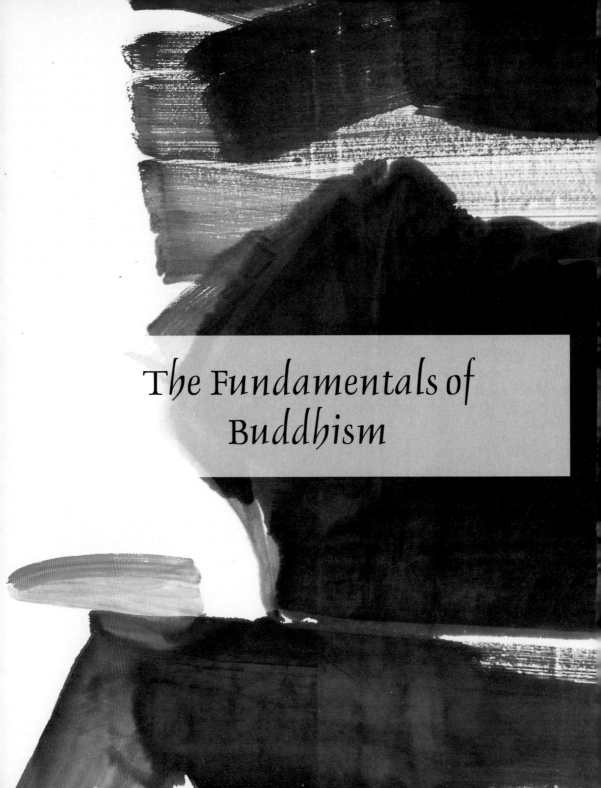

The Fundamentals of Buddhism

The Fundamentals of Buddhism

✤

Those who are blinded by attraction and repulsion cannot comprehend such a Doctrine which goes against the grain, is subtle, profound and difficult to define.

Majhimanikaja

IN ORDER TO UNDERSTAND Zen Buddhism properly it is important to know something about Buddhism itself. The ultimate experience for a Buddhist is the realization of *Nirvāna (Nibbana)* which releases one from the addictions and consequences of *dukkha*, or suffering. No one can describe this experience because it is ineffable. It was in this condition of inner freedom that the Buddha dwelt after his Enlightenment.

It was only after years of study and contemplation that the Buddha achieved the state of Enlightenment.

Nibbana have I realized, and gazed into the mirror
Of the Dharma, the Noble Truth,
I am healed of my wound;
Down is my burden laid; My task is done
My heart is utterly set free.

John Hick, *Death and Eternal Life*

In a state of Nirvāna a person is no longer dominated by the desires or fears which arise from clinging to illusions about life. This absolute inner freedom is experienced as a state of tranquil joy.

In the Buddha's time, *Nirvāna* was seen as the search for identifying and liberating a person's true self. The Buddha taught that within a conventional, empirical self there is no permanent, substantial independent, metaphysical self. For the Buddha, a 'person' was a 'connection of rapidly changing and interacting mental and physical processes, with character-patterns reoccurring over some time. Only partial control can be exercised over these processes, and so they often change in undesired ways, leading to suffering. Impermanent, they cannot be a permanent self.'[1]

Buddhists believe in a cycle of birth, death and rebirth (karma)
which is broken only when Nirvāna is reached.

The Noble Truths

Buddhism has no need to postulate a permanent self. It accounts for the functioning of personality in life, and from life to life, in terms of changing, conditioned processes. The Buddhist analysis of reality is only a means to generate the persuasion that the world we occupy and attribute so much importance to is, in fact, a series of phenomena that are transient and devoid of any permanence (*an-atta*). They are therefore hollow and unsatisfactory (*dukkha*).

The Buddha identified the origin of suffering as the craving, or *tanha*: the search for fulfilment in the here and now is the cause of all our unhappiness. The Buddha also believed that debates about the world, the soul, and man's survival led to endless quarrels and intellectual confusion and he set them aside altogether. This First Noble Truth simply states the fact of suffering – our basic dissatisfaction, alienation and loneliness. The Second Noble Truth identifies the cause of the suffering – our craving and despising, attachments and aversions, all born of our ignorance which prevents us realizing our 'Buddha-nature'. The Third Noble Truth states that liberation from all clinging induces complete peace or *Nirvāna*. The Fourth Noble Truth is the 'Eightfold Path' that leads to liberation. The Eightfold Path consists of correct views, correct thought, correct speech, correct action, correct livelihood, correct effort, correct mindfulness, and correct *Samadhi*. The latter is understood as a state of mind characterized by one-pointedness of attention; a non-dualistic state of awareness.

The Four Noble Truths are the essential truths of Buddhism. There is another essential element in Buddhism, however, and it is termed rebirth.

The state of Nirvāna is a freedom from suffering, an escape from the endless cycle.

The harbour of refuge, the cool cave, the island amidst the floods, the place of bliss, emancipation, liberation, safety, the supreme, the transcendental, the uncreated, the tranquil, the home of ease, the calm. The end of suffering, the medicine for all evil, the unshaken, the ambrosia, the immaterial, the imperishable, the abiding, the further shore, the unending, the bliss of effort, the supreme joy, the ineffable, the detachment, the holy city.

Rhys Davids, Early Buddhism
(Descriptive phrases of Buddhism from ancient scriptures)

Rebirth

Buddhists believe in a continuation of our life of birth and death in accordance with our behaviour on earth. The understanding here is that the law of action and reaction (*karma*) is operative, and what one sows, one will also reap, now or in a later life. Human beings are part of a continuous existence of a universe which springs from one deathless source and, in time, they return to that source to be emitted once more. As part of such a system, humanity as a whole, is ultimately deathless. When the body breaks up, it carries on its existence as an element in the universe. There is also in the human being something which shares the nature of the source, indeed is the source, untouched by time and death in a universal context. An individual's death, therefore, is not regarded as the end of life, but rather a part of the life and death state which persists as long as we fail to achieve *Nirvāna*.

The Road to **Nirvāna**

According to the Buddhist scholar Richard Gombrich, a great many Western writers have consistently misunderstood the concept of *Nirvāna*, assuming that it is little more than 'the blowing out' of the person or soul.[2] This is a Buddhist heresy, he claims, and the entire process of reaching *Nirvāna* is far more involved. One must extinguish the thirst for greed, hatred and delusion. By meditational discipline, a person experiences the truth first-hand within his/her own body and consciousness. That individual then directly 'realizes' the changing states within the body and consciousness, the momentary rise and disappearance of feelings, thoughts and even consciousness itself. Finally, there is the full 'going out' in *Nirvāna*. *Nirvāna* is not a 'thing', but the experience of being without

Buddhists must strive to experience Enlightenment through self-examination, contemplation, and meditation.

greed, hatred and delusion. The poems of Enlightened monks and nuns describe it as blissfully peaceful and cool. That such an experience is possible was demonstrated by the Buddha's own analysis; that it is attainable was shown by his example. The Buddha told his followers to 'live as islands', to be 'their own resorts'. He called upon his followers to embark on a painstaking, practical training through meditation in order to arrive at an understanding of suffering and thus to escape from it.

Sila, Samadhi and Panna

The lower level, or first stage, on the road to *Nirvāna* is called *Sila* which may be roughly translated as 'morality'. *Sila* refers primarily to those external standards of behaviour that represent minimal Buddhist morality for the layman or woman. The core of *Sila* is the Five Precepts which serve as a basic moral code for the individual and society. They are primarily concerned with the prohibition of anti-social actions – killing, stealing, lying, sexual aggression and intoxication – and if positively adopted as principles by an individual, they make for a sober and responsible member of society. To reach *Nirvāna*, a person's life must be based on a good ethical foundation, although the process is not spoken of in terms of ethical standards, but rather in terms of a mystical experience.

Above the level of the *Sila* there is *Samadhi* – the power of mental concentration, the attainment of one-pointedness of mind. Above this level again, there is *Panna*, or what might also be described as insight and wisdom – the crown of the Enlightened life.

Nirvāna has many qualitative implications, but there is no substantial statement to capture its whole essence, and Buddhism is especially insistent on its indescribability. It might, however, be understood as the extinction of hatred, greed and delusion, or the consummation of the *an-atta*, the 'no-self' doctrine.

The doctrine and discipline which I have imparted to you, will be your leader when I am gone. Try hard to reach the goal.

Buddha's Last Words

The Middle Way

Progress towards *Nirvāna* may be portrayed as the progressive realization of the emptiness of all selfhood. Prince Siddhartha, who was later to be known as the Buddha (b. *circa* 565 BC), taught a gradual way of self-discipline, in which he indicated a method of coming to terms with deep-seated tendencies and mental habits common to every life. The Way begins by developing a strong desire to take refuge in the Buddha, the *Dharma* (teachings), and *Sanga* (the community). Through the process of awareness, humans can achieve an absolute liberty, a loving wisdom which is infinite, free from both life and death.

The Buddha offered a radical redefinition of the nature and goal of existence to men and women troubled by the instability of an age of transition. His teaching consisted neither in the sort of empirical analysis we might require today (though it was replete with shrewd observations, not only on the vagaries of human nature, but also on economics and politics), nor in the metaphysical speculations so fondly explored by his contemporaries. He referred to his teaching simply as *Dharma*, an untranslatable word whose meanings range from 'idea', to 'reality and truth', to 'law' and 'righteousness'. It focused essentially on a practice of meditation, on the explanations necessary for understanding and carrying it out,

Overleaf: *The poems of Enlightened monks and nuns describe Nirvāna as blissfully peaceful and cool.*

and on an accompanying ethical code.[3] The Buddha's theories were handed down orally for more than five centuries until, eventually, they were preserved in literary form in the *pitakas*, or doctrinal sermons, and in the *vinaya*, or the monastic discipline.

The Real Permanent

The more one realizes the unreality of the world and of oneself, the more one will come to realize the reality of *Nirvāna* – the Real Permanent. In Buddhist thought, reality is the complete negation of change. *Nirvāna*, as the great Primordial Simple – that which has no parts, no distinctions within it and is eternally the same. This indeed is the only way in which Buddhism knows how to define reality; that which changes, it views as necessarily unreal.[4]

The other implication of *Nirvāna* as the Real Permanent is that it is impersonal. Yet in this sense it is paradoxical, for *Nirvāna* is both highly personal and individual on the one hand, while on the other, it is the negation of all that is personal and individual. A person's experience of *Nirvāna* is within the depths of his being; it is achieved by his own efforts and for himself. Although when realized, it affects the body, it is essentially a state of mind, an indescribable experience which cannot be shared.

This state of *Nirvāna* should not be taken as sheer negation, even though it may appear as such. As King explains it: 'Though the self ceases to "exist", and though *Nirvāna* may be "the graveyard of the mind" and the cessation of consciousness, it is nonetheless infinitely desirable, the one legitimate object of man's passionate striving, with heart, "soul", mind and strength.'[5]

Opposite: *The essence of Nirvāna cannot be explained literally, but it is understood to be a feeling of emptiness, an achievement of the 'no-self' doctrine.*
Overleaf: *The Buddhist philosophy offered a new meaning and point of existence to people in a time of change.*

Of what I know, I have told you only a little....
And why have I not told you the rest?
Because it would not help lead you to Nirvāna.

Buddha, on the subject of Nirvāna

Any attempt to provide a coherent, rational elucidation of the concept of final *Nirvāna* bears little satisfaction. As far as the individual practitioner of Buddhism is concerned, final *Nirvāna* is completely beyond rational elucidation, and must simply be taken on trust.

1   Peter Harvey, *An Introduction to Buddhism: Teachings, History and Practices*, Cambridge 1990.
2   Richard Gombrich, *Theravada Buddhism: A Social History From Ancient Benares to Modern Colombo*, London 1988.
3   John D'arcy May, Meaning, *Consensus and Dialogue in Buddhist-Christian Communication*, New York 1984.
4   Winston L. King, *In the Hope of Nibbana*, Illinois 1964
5   Ibid, p. 87.

The Buddha taught only what was necessary for followers to know to find their own way to Enlightenment.

What is Zen?

What is Zen?

O Supreme Eternal Reality, Pure Being beyond all subject and object, beyond all cerebral thinking, Unconceptualizable and Unverbalizable, dwelling in silence. I long to experience the nameless, incomprehensible being, as Moses did at the Burning Bush, burning and never consumed, a higher consciousness, before which I can only bow in silence and reverence, glimpsing indescribably suchness and eternal mystery.

Anon. A Christian tries to pray in Zen terms, from The Oxford Book of Prayer

THE PRACTICE OF ZEN has as its aim the purification, deepening and transformation of the consciousness. It seeks to realize the mind of the Buddha through za-zen or sitting meditation. Za is understood as 'sitting' and zen is Samadhi, meaning one-pointedness of attention. Hakuin Zenji (1685–1768), one of the most powerful and influential Patriarchs of Japanese Rinzai Zen, through whom all present day masters of Rinzai have their lineage, is said to have valued za-zen highly, insisting that 'no praise can exhaust its merits'. Dogen Zenji of the Soto Zen lineage declared that, 'The Way of the Buddhas and Patriarchs is nothing but za-zen. Do not pursue anything else.'

When you practise za-zen, don't make any conjectures on good and evil. Don't try to stop your thoughts from coming. Ask yourself only this question: 'Which is my own spirit?'

Bassui

Basic Practice

The basic exercise of Zen involves sitting in a traditional Japanese posture, with the feet drawn up underneath the body, and breathing correctly for the purpose of meditation. This elementary Zen exercise leads to certain mental accomplishments, one of which is silence. Zen is a silent meditation and its silence embraces the entire person. Practitioners must give themselves passively to meditation, in complete detachment, and follow only the direction of the master. In this deep meditative practice the mind empties itself of all elements of thought, concept and images.

Zen meditation does not invite the practitioner to focus on a given object. Dogen, the founder of the Japanese Soto school of Zen Buddhism, insisted on this basic aspect of meditation. In his writing, *General Teachings for the Promotion of Za-zen*, he instructs his followers to 'Give up looking for explanations and chasing words! Learn to turn the light back on yourself and to let it shine on your own nature.'

Overleaf: *The practice of Zen aims to purify, deepen and, ultimately, transform the consciousness of the individual.*

Because *Nirvāna* is the only Real Permanent, Dogen advocated the forgetting of objects. The classic text for the definition of *za-zen* as non-thinking, freed from all objects, is found in the *koan*-like dialogue, often cited by Dogen, between a Chinese master of the Tang period and his disciple:

As the great master Yueh-shan hung-tao sat quietly, a monk asked him: 'Of what does one think while sitting?'
The master replied: 'One thinks of not-thinking.'
To this the monk replied: 'How does man think of not-thinking?'
The master: 'Without thinking.'

With this understanding of objectless meditation, the Buddhist teaching on non-self comes into play. The person who meditates in this manner is released from thinking, desiring, craving and clinging. He becomes independent of all things and begins to forget the ego.

Stages of Meditation

In Zen there are four stages of meditation enabling one to remove delusions and achieve bliss in the world of form. During the first stage, five states of mind – investigation, reflection, joyfulness, bliss, and a concentrated state of mind – are realized. They are accompanied by eight types of feelings and ten virtues. In the second stage, there are four states of mind – serenity, joyfulness, bliss, and a concentrated state of mind. The third stage is characterized by five states of mind – equanimity, remembrance, wisdom, bliss, and a concentrated state of mind. The fourth stage has four states of mind – neither suffering nor joy, equanimity, remembrance, and a concentrated state of mind. The Zen practitioner is someone who seeks guidance from a master in order to learn this method of objectless meditation.

Zen Buddhists meditate in a traditional Japanese sitting position, which aids correct breathing and mental detachment.

A principal means of reaching *satori* (Enlightenment) is through the use of *koans*, a series of paradoxical exchanges between master and student designed to radically transform the student's way of thinking, by teaching him to abandon purely logical thought.

The Koan

> **If you meet someone in the street who has reached the truth, you may neither walk past him in silence, nor speaking. How then should you meet him?**

A typical koan

The *koan* is of Chinese origin and testifies to the creative power of the old masters and their methods of teaching. Approximately seventeen hundred *koans* have been recorded from the Chinese and Japanese sources. Many of these recount an exchange between master and student or a master's Enlightenment experience and are known as 'case *koans*'. They can be found in various collections, including *Momonkan* (*The Gateless Gate*), *Hekigan Roku* (*The Blue Cliff Record*), *Shoyo Roku* (*The Book of Equanimity*) and *Denko Roku* (*The Book of the Transmission of the Lamp*). It must be remembered that *koan* practice is merely a method which is intimately connected with the essence of Zen.

There are four stages of meditation, each one characterized by varying states of mind.

A student of the Rinzai School of Zen in Japan is expected to pass a series of about fifty *koan* problems and publication of the acceptable answers to the problems is forbidden. The point of the exercise is that the *koan* is given to the student as an object of study and practice in order that he/she will so completely appropriate it that it no longer stands as a separate object. To find the solution of the *koan* means becoming one with it. The *koan* system, as we know it today, is mainly the work of Hakuin.

Nowadays, a true follower of Zen must submit himself to a complete course of Zen study which is divided into six stages (the first five of which centre on mastering the *koans*):

1. Hosshin, or *Dharmakaya koan* – whereby one 'enters into the frontier gate of Zen'.
2. Kikan, or 'cunning barrier' *koan* – which deals with the active expression of the state realized in the first group.
3. Gonzen, or 'investigation of words' *koan* – which has to do with the expression of Zen understanding in speech and dialogue.
4. Nanto, or 'hard to penetrate' *koan*.
5. Goi, or 'Five Ranks' *koan* – based on the five relationships of 'lord' and 'servant', or of 'principle' and 'thing-event', wherein Zen is related to the *Hua-yen or Avatamsaka* philosophy. This philosophy is based on the *Avatamsaka Suttra*, which is the final culmination of Indian Mahayana Buddhism. This doctrine explores the theory that harmony of the universe is realized when each 'thing-event' is allowed to be itself.
6. The sixth and final stage is the study of the precepts of Buddhism and the regulation of the monk's life according to Zen understanding.[2]

Students of Zen are expected to master the koans – problems or riddles with no one correct answer, but many interpretations.

A Zen monk wishing to embrace the *koan* system completely will devote about thirty years of his life to them.

1   Dumoulin, Heinrich, *Zen Buddhism in the 20th Century*, Tokyo 1992.
2   This outline is based on information presented by Ruth Saaki during
     a conference at the American Academy of Asian Studies.

A Zen monk undergoes six stages of study, including how his own life is regulated according to the precepts of Buddhism.

Hsin-hsin Ming

Hsin-*h*sin Ming

✤

HSIN-HSIN MING IS THE TITLE of an ancient poem dating from the seventh century, and is considered to be the first comprehensive statement of Zen. Consisting of one hundred and forty-six four-word lines written entirely in Chinese, without Sanskrit, it is said to have been the work of Seng-ts'an (c. AD 606), the Third Patriarch of Zen in China. According to the Buddhist scholar Dennis Merzel, the title of the poem is 'the verbal expression of the fact that the very nature of existence and of all the phenomenal world are none other than the faith mind.' [1] This 'faith', however, is not to be understood as faith in something, but is the very fact of existence, or reality itself. *Satori*, or Enlightenment, is the term used for this 'faith' in Japanese Zen, where no differentiation exists between practice and Enlightenment, and vice versa. The word 'mind' is best interpreted in this instance as 'consciousness' – a state of awareness or consciousness of the one true reality which is equated with *Satori*.

From the time of its original composition, up until the present day, *Hsin-hsin Ming* has been published and translated by various scholars both in China and Japan. The founder of the Japanese Soto School, Dogen Zenji, quoted from *Hsin-hsin Ming* in his *Eihei-koroku*, which was written in Chinese. Again, in 1303, Keizan Zenji, the co-founder of the Japanese Soto School, wrote commentaries on some verses of *Hsin-hsin Ming* and in the Edo period (eighteenth century), Kozan Garyu also wrote a commentary on the verses. In modern times there have been several Japanese commentaries on this poem, among the most famous of which is that by Kodo Sawaki Roshi.

The first verse of *Hsin-hsin Ming* states the challenge to acquire the bodhi, or the awakened mind of the Buddha. To achieve this, we should not indulge preferences. We should free ourselves of all likes and dislikes.

> *The Great Way is not difficult*
> *for those who have no preferences.*
> *When love and hate are both absent*
> *everything becomes clear and undisguised.*
> *Make the smallest distinction, however,*
> *and heaven and earth are set infinitely apart.*

When we sit and meditate and allow everything to be just as it is without loving it or hating it, we then invite harmony. That is the way of the Tao – a simple, unforced way of living, with no conflict with the natural laws – the fundamental order of the universe.

> *The Way is perfect like vast space*
> *where nothing is lacking and nothing is in excess.*
> *Indeed, it is due to our choosing to accept or reject*
> *that we do not see the true nature of things.*
> *Live neither in the entanglements of outer things,*
> *nor in the inner feeling of emptiness.*

It is not so easy, however, to sit and meditate, for we have a continual flow of thoughts invading our consciousness. In Zen practice it is necessary to give up every effort to stop thinking. We must let go and trust.

Overleaf: Many ancient writings and scriptures expound the knowledge and teachings of Buddhism.

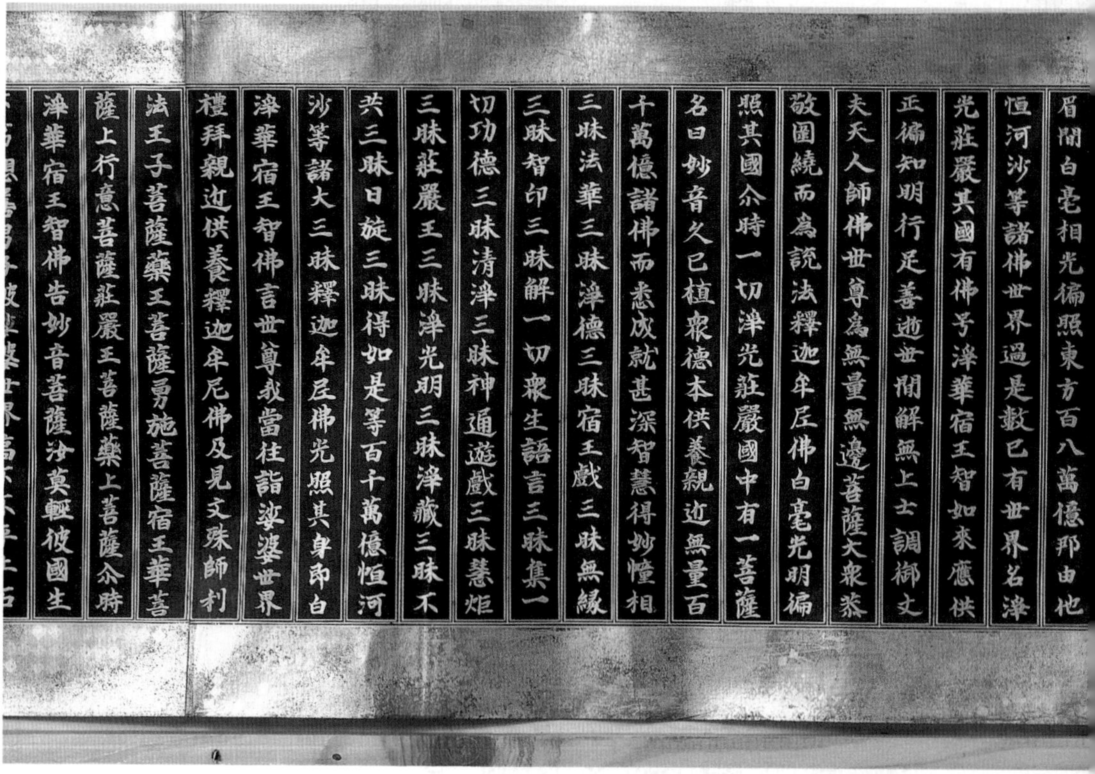

眉間白毫相光徧照東方百八萬億那由他

恒河沙等諸佛世界過是數已有世界名淨

光莊嚴其國有佛号淨華宿王智如來應供

正徧知明行足善逝世間解無上士調御丈

夫天人師佛世尊為無量無邊菩薩大衆恭

敬圍繞而為說法釋迦牟尼佛白毫光明徧

照其國尒時一切淨光莊嚴國中有一菩薩

名曰妙音久已植衆德本供養親近無量百

千萬億諸佛而悉成就甚深智慧得妙幢相

三昧法華三昧淨德三昧宿王戲三昧無緣

三昧智印三昧解一切衆生語言三昧集一

切功德三昧清淨三昧神通遊戲三昧慧炬

三昧莊嚴王三昧淨光明三昧淨藏三昧不

共三昧日旋三昧得如是等百千萬億恒河

沙等諸大三昧釋迦牟尼佛光照其身即白

淨華宿王智佛言世尊我當往詣娑婆世界

禮拜親近供養釋迦牟尼佛及見文殊師利

法王子菩薩藥王菩薩勇施菩薩宿王華菩

薩上行意菩薩莊嚴王菩薩藥上菩薩众時

淨華宿王智佛告妙音菩薩汝莫輕彼國生

Those who do not live in the single Way
fail in both activity and in passivity,
assertion and denial.
To deny the reality of things
is to miss their reality.
The more you talk and think about it,
the further astray you wander from the truth.
Stop talking and thinking
and there is nothing you will not be able to know.

Most people seek out truth in the phenomenal world, in external things, assuming they will find happiness in material comfort, power, fame and position. The way to Enlightenment is to know that eventually these things bring us neither happiness nor truth. We tend to construct our own realities and channel our energies into holding them together, in what we call 'life'. Only when we let go of our striving is it possible to enter within ourselves and discover the truth.

Do not remain in the dualistic state;
avoid such pursuits carefully.
If there is even a trace
of this and that, of right and wrong,
the Mind-essence will be lost in confusion.
Although all dualities come from the One,
do not be attached even to this one.
When the mind exists undisturbed in the Way,
nothing in the world can offend,
it ceases to exist in the old way.

The way to Enlightenment lies in the realization that truth
and happiness cannot be found in the external world.

Zen embraces a profound philosophy of self-awakening and
freedom from man's egocentric perception of the world.

All our problems have their origin in the perception of ourselves as separate entities. *Hsin-hsin Ming* challenges us to stop clinging to our opinions and personal preferences because we are fearful. Freedom is the greatest gift of all. The mind is the instrument which creates our whole world, but we will always feel separate if we continue to be egocentric in our perception of it. The path to the discovery of our true selves lies in complete openness to each moment of life. There is no need for discrimination.

> To live in the Great Way
> is neither easy nor difficult.
> But those with limited views
> are fearful and irresolute:
> the faster they hurry, the slower they go.
> Clinging cannot be limited;
> even to be attached to the idea of Enlightenment.

The nature of things is called emptiness or Buddha-nature, and this in turn is no-nature. Our true essence is no-thingness.

> If you wish to move in the One Way
> do not dislike even the world of senses and ideas.
> Indeed, to accept them fully
> is identical with true Enlightenment.
> The wise man strives to no goals
> but the foolish man fetters himself.
> There is one Dharma, not many;
> distinctions arise from clinging needs of the ignorant.
> To seek Mind with discriminating mind
> is the greatest of all mistakes.

There is only one truth, one reality and it is the life you hold, yourself, the way things are. We try to alter circumstances to improve the quality of our lives, but a person is *Dharma*, the living truth. This must include everything and we should never try to avoid what we consider the unpleasant in life, but face it willingly, and strive to be one with it.

> Rest and unrest derive from illusions;
> with Enlightenment there is no liking and disliking.
> All dualities come from ignorant inference.
> They are like dreams of flowers in air;
> foolish to try to grasp them.
> Gain and loss, right and wrong:
> such thoughts must finally be abolished at once.

When we are still and motionless there is perfect balance. At this moment we become aware of our transparent and formless nature and we experience our emptiness.

> To come directly into harmony with this reality
> just simply say when doubt arises 'Not two'.
> In this 'not two' nothing is separate,
> nothing is excluded.
> No matter when or where,
> Enlightenment means entering this truth.
> And this truth is beyond extension or diminution in time or space;
> in it a single thought is ten thousand years.

'This truth is beyond extension or diminution in time or space
in it a single thought is ten thousand years.' (Hsin-hsin Ming)

The world we live in is empty of meaning and an awareness of this truth will allow us rebirth. While meditating, we let go of all our definitions of life and we break free.

One thing, all things:
move among and intermingle,
without distinction.
To live in this realization
is to be without anxiety about non-perfection.
To live in this faith is the road to non-duality,
because the non-dual is one with the trusting mind.

Monastic Life

Although Zen asserts that Enlightenment can be found just as much by working in the world as in withdrawing from it, monastic life has always been of crucial importance, as it has to all schools of Buddhism. The Bodhisattva Nagarjuna, who was one of the chief philosophers of Mahayana Buddhism, asked himself what merit there was in becoming a monk. He answered his own question, saying: 'Although it is true that both laymen and monks can realize Enlightenment, there is a difference in the relative difficulty each encounters. Because laymen have to make a living, it is difficult for them to devote themselves to Buddhist training . . . . On the other hand, it is much easier for monks, being free of worldly responsibilities, anger, and various distractions, to devote them-selves to the practice of Buddhism.'

Opposite: *A Bodhisattva has attained spiritual perfection,*
but delays his reward of Nirvāna to work towards the salvation of others.
Overleaf: *Zen expresses a reality which is beyond negation and affirmation, speech and silence.*

Within the monastery, monks show complete obedience to the *Dharma Father*. Monastic life is regulated, and the new monk must learn to adapt. As a novice he works in the house, the temple and the garden, cleaning cooking and pruning. Each monk is allotted one *tatami* or mat, where he eats, sleeps, sits and meditates. The community of monks have two meals a day and nothing is eaten after midday. A monk is allowed very few personal belongings, since Buddhism teaches that possession is one of the worst cravings.

There is a period in the monastic life that is set aside for the mental discipline of the monks and this period is known as *sesshin*. It takes place in summer and in winter. In his book, *An Introduction to Zen Buddhism*, D. T. Suzuki states that there is a lecture every day during the *sesshin*. The textbook used may be any of the Zen books such as the *Hekiganshu*, or the *Mumonkwan*, each of them a collection of *koans*. The *Kidoroku*, which contains sayings, sermons, poems and other works by Kido (Hsu-t'ang) of the Sung dynasty. Besides the lectures there is *sanzen*, a period when monks present their views on the *koans* to their master.

The monks chant the four vows of Zen as an expression of their aspiration, and their lives are a symbol of harmony through the discipline of work and meditation. The monastery is a microcosm of the human social organization, devoted to the practice of the Buddhist Way. A monk willingly renounces cravings and desires to achieve Enlightenment, but not just for himself alone. Zen does not permit the life of a hermit, isolated from reality and the complexity of the problems associated with it. The monk identifies himself with the problems of the world of sentient beings, and by following the Way, points to the solution to alleviate the suffering of others.

Opposite: In a monastery, such as this, the Eihei-Ji monastery, a monk can devote all his time to Buddhist training, because he has no worldly responsibilities or distractions
Overleaf: Each monk has his own tatami on which he eats, sleeps, sits and meditates.

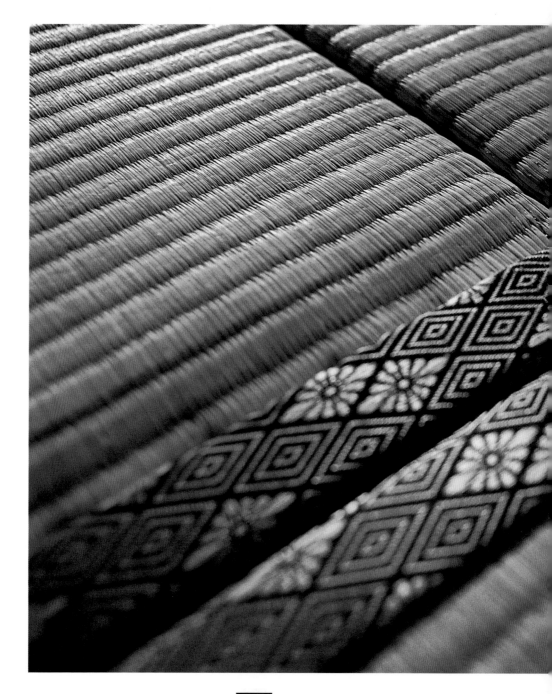

Those who enter the gate of Buddhism should first of all cherish a firm faith in the dignity and respectability of monkhood, for it is the path leading them away from poverty and humbleness .... When the monk finds himself in this position of dignity and respectability, living in the rock-cave of the Dharma where he enjoys the greatest happiness of a spiritual life, under the blissful protection of all the guardian gods of the Triple Treasure, is there any form of happiness that can surpass his?

Last words of the monk, Dai-o Kokush, from the translation by Dr D. T. Suzuki

Opposite: *The happiness experienced by a monk living a spiritual life according to the laws of Dharma, is unsurpassable.*
Overleaf: *Zen Buddhism does not allow monks to live in isolation — they interact with people in their everyday lives.*

The Significance of Zen in Contemporary Life

Buddhism does not speak of the one God, but of emptiness and, as such, is often misunderstood as something negative. Emptiness in Buddhism, however, is not a nihilistic emptiness, but a non-dualistic form, wherein all particular things are just as they are and are equal. Zen Buddhism, in fact, does not negate human desire, but seeks to transcend the duality of pleasure and suffering by adopting the Middle Way. To live the Middle Way is to achieve *Nirvāna*, which in turn is to be truly Enlightened, to discover our original Buddha-nature.

The influence of Zen on Far Eastern culture is extremely difficult to measure. Suffice it to say that Zen has left its mark on every area of life, and it is estimated that there are currently over ten million followers of Zen Buddhism in Japan alone, divided between the Soto and Rinzai schools. The advent of Zen in the West has led to a multiplicity of theological hypotheses and practical forms of spiritual exercise. In an age of restless movement and stress, *za-zen* teaches silent meditation and offers a philosophy of life to rouse the individual from the rut of day-to-day existence. Heinrich Dumoulin provides a most incisive statement on its importance in his assertion that, 'to Westerners who have lost their equilibrium, Zen teaches an attitude that integrally embraces body and mind and is experienced psychologically as a new consciousness'.[2]

[1]   Dennis Genpo Merzel, *The Eye that Never Sleeps —
Striking to the Heart of Zen*, London 1991.
[2]   Dumoulin, Heinrich, *Zen Buddhism in the 20th Century*, Tokyo 1992.

Above: *The way of the Tao is a simple,
unforced way of living, allowing no conflict with the natural laws.*
Opposite: *Zen has penetrated contemporary life in many ways –
even the gardens of the temples and monasteries are influenced by it.*
Overleaf: *Zen is prevalent in many Japanese crafts from architecture to
painting and drawing.*

Suggested Further Reading

❦

Abe Masao, *Zen and Western Thought*, Hawaii 1985

Brutt, E. A., ed., *The Teachings of the Compassionate Buddha*,
   New York 1955

Conze, Edward; Horner, I. B.; Snellgrove, David; Waley, Arthur, *Buddhist Texts
   Through The Ages*, New York 1954

Dumoulin, Heinrich, *Zen Buddhism in the 20th Century*, Tokyo 1992

Griffiths, Paul, *On Being Mindless, Buddhist Meditation and the Mind-Body Problem*,
   Illinois 1986

Kornfield, Jack, *Living Buddhist Masters*, California 1977

Merton, Thomas, *Mystics & Zen Masters*, New York 1961

Merzel Genpo Dennis, *The Eye Never Sleeps, Striking to the Heart of Zen*,
   London 1991

Suzuki D. T., *An Introduction To Buddhism*, Essex 1949

Watts W. Alan, *The Way Of Zen*, Middlesex 1957

Yokoi Yuho, *Zen Master Dogen: An Introduction With Selected Writings*,
   Tokyo 1976

Illustration Notes

✤

Page 9 *Buddha Meditating by a Waterfall* by Li Ruiqing. Courtesy of Christie's Images. **Page 10** *Mount Fuji: Rainstorm Beneath the Peak* by Katsushika Hokusai. Courtesy of Christie's Images. **Pages 12-13** *Water and Clouds Share the Same Source.* by Liu Guosong. Courtesy of Christie's Images. **Page 15** Detail from *The Sixty-Nine Stations of the Kiso Highway* by Ando Hiroshige. Courtesy of Christie's Images. **Pages 16-17** *Mount Fuji: Rainstorm Beneath the Peak* by Katsushika Hokusai. Courtesy of Christie's Images. **Page 19** *Buddha* by Zhang Daqian. Courtesy of Christie's Images. **Pages 20-1** Detail from *The Sixty-Nine Stations of the Kiso Highway* by Ando Hiroshige. Courtesy of Christie's Images. **Page 23** *Bodhidarma.* Courtesy of Circa Photo Library. **Pages 24-5** *Eihei-Ji Monastery.* Courtesy of Axiom Photographic Agency. **Page 27** *Painting of Mount Hiei and Zen Temples.* Courtesy of Jim Holmes/Axiom Photographic Agency. **Pages 28-9** *Zen Painting: Bold Strokes* by Lu Shoukun. Courtesy of Christie's Images. **Page 31** *Buddha Meditating by a Waterfall* by Li Ruiqing. Courtesy of Christie's Images. **Page 33** *Wheel of Life.* Courtesy of the MacQuitty International Collection. **Page 34** *Mountains and Rivers of Kiso* by Ando Hiroshige. Courtesy of Christie's Images. **Page 37** *Monk Meditation.* Courtesy of Axiom Photographic Agency. **Pages 40-1** Detail from *Buddhist Painting Showing the Bodhisattva Samanthabhadra on a Lotus Base on an Elephant.* Courtesy of Christie's Images. **Page 43** Detail from *Full Moon* by Liu Guosong. Courtesy of Christie's Images. **Pages 44-5** *Onon Waterfall the Kiso Highway* by Katsushika Hokusai. Courtesy of Christie's Images. **Page 47** *Buddhist Painting Showing the Bodhisattva Samanthabhadra on a Lotus Base on an Elephant.* Courtesy of Christie's Images. **Pages 48-9** *Onon Waterfall the Kiso Highway* by Katsushika Hokusai. Courtesy of Christie's Images. **Pages 52-3** *Screen from Koto-In Zen Garden, Daitokuji Temple.* Courtesy of Jim Holmes/Axiom Photographic Agency. **Page 55** *Large Cypress Wood Sculpture* of Amida Nyorai. Courtesy of Christie's Images. **Page 56** *Scholar Composing Under a Pine Tree* by Huang Janbi. Courtesy of Christie's Images. **Page 59** *Monk at Koto-In Zen Garden, Daitokuji Temple.* Courtesy of Jim Holmes/Axiom Photographic Agency. **Page 60** Detail from *Buddha* by Zhang Daqian. Courtesy of Christie's Images. **Page 61** *Koto-In Zen Garden, Daitokuji Temple.* Courtesy of Jim Holmes/Axiom Photographic Agency. **Pages 62-3** *Reclining Buddha at Dazu* by Wu Guanzhong. Courtesy of Christie's Images. **Pages 66-7** *The Lotus Sutra.* Courtesy of Christie's Images. **Page 69** Detail from *Full Moon* by Liu Guosong. Courtesy of Christie's Images. **Page 70** *Peacefulness* by Zhou Luyun. Courtesy of Christie's Images. **Page 73** Detail from *Peacefulness* by Zhou Luyun. Courtesy of Christie's Images. **Page 75** *Large Gilt-Bronze Figure of a Bodhisattva.* Courtesy of Christie's Images. **Pages 76-7** Detail from *Buddhist Palace in Tibet* by Jiang Mingxian. Courtesy of Christie's Images. **Page 78** *Eihei-Ji Monastery.* Courtesy of Jim Holmes/Axiom Photographic Agency. **Pages 80-1** *Traditional Rush Made Tatami Floor Mats.* Courtesy of Jim Holmes/Axiom Photographic Agency. **Page 83** *Buddhist Palace in Tibet* by Jiang Mingxian. Courtesy of Christie's Images. **Pages 84-5** *Monk Collecting Alms in Kyoto.* Courtesy of Jim Holmes/Axiom Photographic Agency. **Page 86** *Zen garden at Ginkakuji Temple.* Courtesy of Jim Holmes/Axiom Photographic Agency. **Page 87** Detail from *Mount Fuji: Rainstorm Beneath the Peak* by Katsushika Hokusai. Courtesy of Christie's Images. **Pages 88-9** Detail from *Buddhist Painting Showing the Bodhisattva Samanthabhadra on a Lotus Base on an Elephant.* Courtesy of Christie's Images.

Index

❄

Index